THE WINTER GAMES

HISTORY OF THE GAMES

The first games were held in 776 B.C. in Olympia, Greece. These first games were dedicated to Zeus, king of the gods. From this point on, the games were held every four years (which has come to be known as an "Olympiad.")

Olympia had large, beautiful temples dedicated to Zeus and Hera alongside the gymnasium and palaestra (the wrestling school). Olympia was the main meeting place for all religious and political activities in Ancient Greece. The stadium in Olympia could hold thousands of people, who would come from all over Greece to see the athletes compete.

During the games, Ancient Greece followed a truce which allowed athletes and spectators to travel safely from their home countries to the games in Olympia. There was no fighting before, during, or after the games to ensure safety of all participants.

Check an atlas or the Internet, and label the location of Olympia. Color Greece, and label the Aegean Sea, Ionian Sea and Mediterranean Sea.

THE FIRST ATHLETES

Fill in the blanks using these words: wreaths, male, youth, woman, chariot, olive, Rome, Kroton, rumored, victory

During the ancient games, athletes had to be three things. They had to be _____, from Greece, and born free. After Greece was conquered by _____, Romans were allowed to join in the games as well. Winners were given _____ made of olive branches to wear on their heads and were treated as heroes when they returned home.

ASTYLOS OF KROTON- Astylos was a runner who won six victory _____ wreaths in three different Olympiads. After his first Olympiad, he competed for Syracuse instead of Kroton, so the people of _____ became angry and destroyed his statue.

MILON OF KROTON- Milon was a wrestling champion and one of the most famous ancient Olympians. He won first as a _____, and then went on to compete five more time as an adult.

KYNISKA OF SPARTA- Kyniska was the first _____ to be listed as an victor. She did not compete, but she owned the horse who won the _____ race, and the owner, not the rider, was listed as the victor.

LEONIDAS OF RHODES- Leonidas is a famous runner. He ran in three different events in four different Olympiads, winning a total of 12 _____ wreaths.

MELANKOMAS OF KARIA- Melankomas was a boxer, who was said to win his matches without ever being hit or hitting anyone else. It is _____ that he won a match by holding his arms out for two days without lowering them, exhausting his opponent.

HISTORY AND ART

After more than a thousand years of games, Emperor Theodosius I converted to Christianity and abolished the games because he did not want people to be worshiping Zeus. Over time, Olympia was destroyed by vandals, earthquakes, and floods.

In 1766, German archaeologists discovered the site of the original games and uncovered the ruins. When someone won an event and returned home, they would often have a statue erected in their home town, as well as find themselves in scenes carved into buildings, and painted on walls and pottery. These pieces of art help tell the story of the victors.

Imagine your home town built a statue in honor of you. What would your statue be of? Where would it be displayed?

_____

_____

_____

_____

_____

SPORTS PLAYED IN OLYMPIA

RUNNING - short "sprints" and longer races

WRESTLING and BOXING

PANKRATION- a type of martial arts that combines boxing and wrestling

CHARIOT and HORSE RACES

PENTATHLON - running, long jump, javelin, discus and wrestling.

BOYS' EVENTS- running, boxing and wrestling

DESIGN YOUR OWN POTTERY

Include scenes of sports, like you may find on Ancient Greek pottery.

GREEK MYTHOLOGY

There are many myths and legends that explain how the games came to be. The most common myth is about Zeus, and how he became king of the gods.

Once, Zeus fought his father, Kronos, for control of the world. Their battle was long and hard. They fought on top of a mountain that over-looked a valley in southwestern Greece. When the battle was over, and Zeus won, a temple and huge statue were built for Zeus as a way to honor him and commemorate the battle.

This valley was called Olympia. The demi-god Hercules staged games of strength there as a way to honor Zeus. Over time, these games became what we know as the modern games.

What else do you know about Zeus? _____

_____

_____

_____

KRONOS   HERCULES   ZEUS

WRITE YOUR OWN HERO STORY

Many Greek myths tell the story of men and women who were stronger and braver than typical humans. Write your own hero story:

_____

_____

_____

_____

_____

_____

_____

_____

_____

_____

_____

_____

_____

_____

_____

_____

_____

_____

_____

WORD SEARCH

Find these words:

RUNNING
WRESTLING
BOXING
PANKRATION
CHARIOT
PENTATHLON
JAVELIN
DISCUS
GYMNASIUM
PALAESTRA
OLYMPIAD
OLYMPIA

ZEUS
HERCULES
KRONOS
ASTYLOS
OLIVE
MILON
KYNISKA
LEONIDAS
MELANKOMAS
GREECE
HERO
ANCIENT

S	Q	P	N	C	U	Y	M	S	C	I	P	M	Y	L	O	U	A	E	X
I	O	A	D	U	O	W	Z	J	P	P	Y	P	U	R	W	S	D	X	A
S	A	A	N	B	W	R	A	K	A	B	O	X	I	N	G	H	W	U	P
U	M	R	H	G	U	V	S	N	J	A	U	A	Y	H	I	O	Q	U	D
C	X	J	K	N	E	C	K	O	G	M	E	L	A	N	K	O	M	A	S
S	W	H	N	L	M	R	J	P	L	D	K	G	U	A	L	K	W	U	H
I	N	I	I	U	A	V	B	I	S	Y	R	C	T	H	A	K	O	A	E
D	N	N	Q	T	N	K	W	F	F	C	M	H	E	X	T	R	W	R	R
G	W	T	I	A	K	S	I	N	Y	K	H	P	K	Y	R	O	R	T	C
C	Q	O	S	G	D	J	Y	G	J	U	L	A	I	K	Y	N	E	S	U
W	N	B	P	L	E	O	N	I	D	A	S	R	R	A	O	O	S	E	L
W	D	C	M	R	N	F	T	A	P	A	H	Q	G	I	D	S	T	A	E
H	N	O	L	H	T	A	T	N	E	P	O	D	C	L	O	A	L	L	S
D	A	D	N	S	E	T	E	V	I	L	O	Z	G	U	L	T	I	A	B
J	S	Z	U	Y	N	O	M	Z	E	R	E	E	T	R	O	U	N	P	I
S	B	L	Q	E	O	L	Y	M	P	I	A	U	U	F	E	R	G	L	Q
M	W	B	I	S	O	L	Y	T	S	A	Y	S	T	T	J	E	E	T	H
M	Q	C	W	Y	I	R	S	Z	B	M	I	L	O	N	C	L	C	H	D
V	N	B	E	L	M	D	M	U	I	S	A	N	M	Y	G	Z	C	E	C
A	G	U	N	Q	K	S	U	Z	F	K	P	E	D	G	H	T	U	S	Z

FUN WITH GREEK ROOTS

Read the root word and its meaning. Then, come up with a word you know that includes the root word. Highlight the root. Use a dictionary or the Internet for help if needed.

ROOT	MEANING	WORDS I KNOW
anthropo	man; human; humanity	_____
auto	self	_____
bio	life	_____
chron	time	_____
dys	bad; hard; unlucky	_____
gram	thing written	_____
hydr	water	_____
hypo	below; beneath	_____
logy	study of	_____
meter/metr	measure	_____
micro	small	_____
mono	one	_____
morph	form; shape	_____
phil	love	_____
phobia	fear	_____
photo/phos	light	_____
therm	heat	_____

THE HISTORY OF THE TORCH

The torch is a tradition that ties the ancient games to the modern games we still hold today.

In ancient times, the people who lived in Athens thought fire was very special. In Greek mythology, the Titan Prometheus stole fire from Zeus. According to the legend, Zeus asked Prometheus to form man out of water and earth. Zeus didn't want humans to have very much power, especially the power over fire.

Prometheus really cared about Humans and wanted them to have many things, but he especially wanted them to have fire and the power it brings. He decided he cared more about mankind than he did about Zeus' wrath, so he stole fire from Zeus' lightning bolt, and he delivered it to mankind.

The Greeks had fires in front of many of their temples and other special places. Fire was so important to them that they believed in keeping it "pure" by lighting it directly from the sun.

Today, the fire used for the torch is still "pure" and lit only by the sun. Before the Winter Games, 11 women gather at the ancient site of the first games in Olympia, Greece, at the Temple of Hera.

They light the fire from the sun using a mirror which concentrates the sun's rays to create heat. This fire is used to light the first torch, which travels around Greece before being handed over to representatives from the country hosting the Winter Games, who complete the relay on their way to the site of the modern games.

BRINGING THE WORLD TOGETHER

Use an atlas or the Internet to help you complete this activity.

1. Color Greece Yellow- Greece is where the games originated and where the torch is lit still today.

2. Label Pyeongchang, South Korea on the map- Pyeongchang is where the Winter Games will be held this year!

3. Color South Korea Blue- the torch traveled all over South Korea before landing in Pyeongchang.

4. Color your home Red- be ready to cheer on the athletes from your country when the Winter Games start!

FOLLOW THE PATH OF THE TORCH

The torch relay takes the torch from Athens (the site of the ancient games, and where the flame is always lit) to its final destination, the location of the games.

This year, since the games are being held in PyeongChang, South Korea, the torch made its way around the whole country so all the Korean people could participate.

In all, the torch traveled 2,018 kilometers from start to finish, and the flame was transferred between 7,500 runners (who represent the 75 million people who call Korea home).

The torch traveled to MANY cities on it's way to PyeongChang. Let's look at some more closely. Find these cities on the map and connect the path of the torch with a line:

1. Incheon
2. Busan
3. Changwon
4. Daejeon
5. Daegu
6. Suwon
7. Seoul
8. PyeongChang

Did you know? The torchbearers are each given their own individual torches. They pass along the flame from one torch to the next during the relay, instead of the torch itself. After their portion of the run, torchbearers are allowed to keep the torch as a memento.

Use an atlas or the Internet to help you map the path of the torch.

SOUTH KOREA

TORCH WORD PROBLEMS

1. The flame traveled a total of 2,018 kilometers. How far is that same distance in miles?

2. 7,500 different torchbearers carried the flame. If each torchbearer carried the flame the same amount of distance, how far would each torchbearer need to carry the flame?

3. There are 75,000,000 people living in Korea. The torch stopped in 45 Korean cities. If an equal number of Korean residents traveled to see the torch at each stop it made (one view per resident), how many people would be watching the torch pass through Incheon on its first stop?

4. The torch relay this year took a total of 109 days! A luge can reach the speed of 140 MPH. If the torch was carried by luge instead of by foot, how long would it take to travel the 2,018 kilometers?

Helpful Hint:
1 mile =
1.6 kilometers

WHO CARRIES THE TORCH?

Many people are selected each year to carry the torch. This year, Korea focused on choosing **Dreamers** and **Achievers** to deliver the torch to the games. Why would you be a good choice to be a torchbearer? Write about your achievements, and what you dream about accomplishing:

_____

_____

_____

_____

_____

_____

_____

_____

_____

_____

_____

_____

_____

_____

_____

_____

_____

_____

_____

_____

THE OFFICIAL TORCH OF 2018

A new torch is designed for each new winter games. This year, the torch has new features designed to help it stay lit while it travels through the extreme weather in South Korea.

Visit the <u>*official 2018 PyeongChang Torch website*</u> *to help you answer these questions.*

1. What does the pentagon shape at the base of the torch represent?

_____

_____

2. What special features does the torch include to help it stay lit?

_____

_____

_____

3. How much wind can the torch withstand?

_____

_____

_____

4. How big is the torch? What does its size represent?

_____

_____

_____

5. What do the stars on the torch represent?

_____

_____

_____

DESIGN YOUR OWN TORCH

Describe your Torch. How big is it? What materials did you use? What does the color and design mean? What special features did you include?

_____

_____

_____

_____

_____

_____

_____

_____

ABOUT SOUTH KOREA

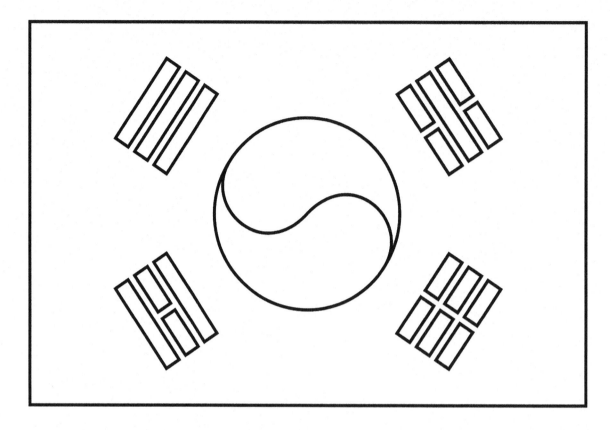

Use an atlas or look on the Internet to help you find the following answers:

Official Name: _____

Type of Government: _____

Capital:_____

Population:_____

Language:_____

Religion:_____

Currency:_____

Tallest Mountain:_____

Important Rivers :_____

Largest City:_____

How large is South Korea? _____

THE KOREAN WAR

Fill in the blanks using these words: million, wildlife, tensions, population, North, countries, safe, communist, isolated, war, border.

The official name of South Korea is "The Republic of Korea" (ROK). South Korea does not acknowledge that _____ Korea is a separate country, despite the _____ between the two nations.

In 1950, _____ forces from North Korea invaded the South, which started the Korean War. Between 1950-1953, more than two and a half _____ people died. The war never officially ended. Instead, a "demilitarized zone" (DMZ) was set up between the _____, and to this day, soldiers from each country stand at that line, prepared for another _____.

The DMZ has become something like a _____ preserve and has been untouched for more than 60 years. Most of the country has buildings because of the large _____ and small size, so this preserved wilderness is important to many people. When the war ends, many people hope to make the DMZ a permanent "peace park."

North Korea is completely _____ from South Korea, and some Korean families have been unable to see or speak to each other for years because no one is allowed to cross the _____ between North and South Korea.

Despite this, South Korea is a very _____ country, and many South Koreans don't worry about the war on a daily basis.

THE OPENING CEREMONY

The opening ceremony is always a carefully guarded secret! You'll be able to see special cultural performances and get your first glimpse of many of the athletes at this ceremony.

Share your favorite part of the opening ceremony:

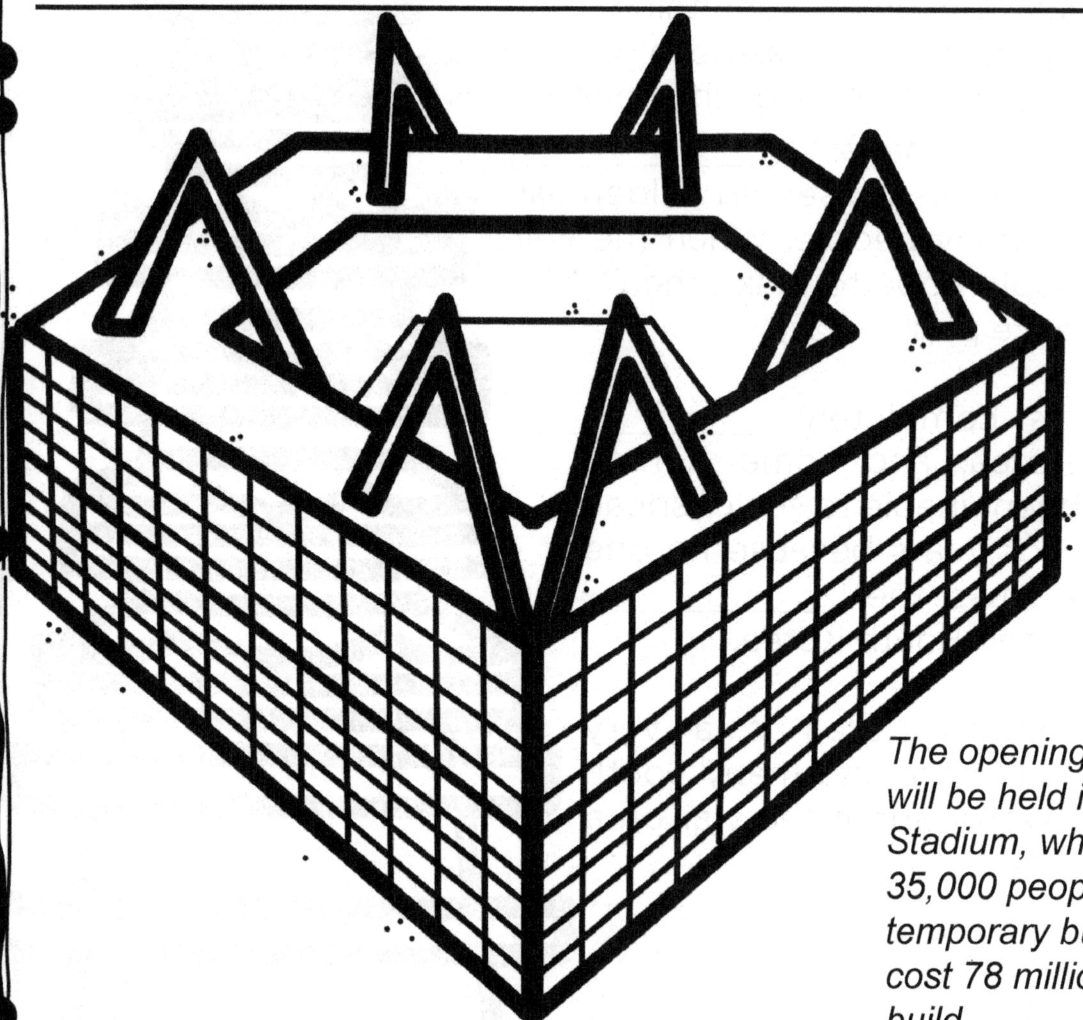

_____

_____

_____

_____

_____

_____

_____

_____

_____

_____

The opening ceremony will be held in the Olympic Stadium, which can seat 35,000 people! This is a temporary building which cost 78 million dollars to build.

GREETINGS AROUND THE WORLD

How to say "Hello" in 20 languages.

Which country would you use these words in?

BONJOUR – French _____

HOLA – Spanish _____

GUTEN TAG – German _____

CIAO – Italian _____

OLÀ – Portuguese _____

NAMASTE – Hindi _____

SALAAM – Persian (Farsi) _____

ZDRAS-TVUY-TE – Russian _____

KONNICHIWA - Japanese _____

AHN-YOUNG-HA-SE-YO – Korean _____

MERHABA – Turkish _____

SAIN BAINUU- Mongolian _____

SALEMETSIZ BE? – Kazakh _____

SZIA – Hungarian _____

MARHABA – Arabic _____

SALAMA ALEIKUM – Hausa _____

JAMBO – Swahili _____

NI HAU – Mandarin _____

NAY HOH – Cantonese (Yue) _____

HALO – Bahasa Indonesia _____

WORLD FLAGS

Color these flags as you see them during the games. Label which country they represent below the flag.

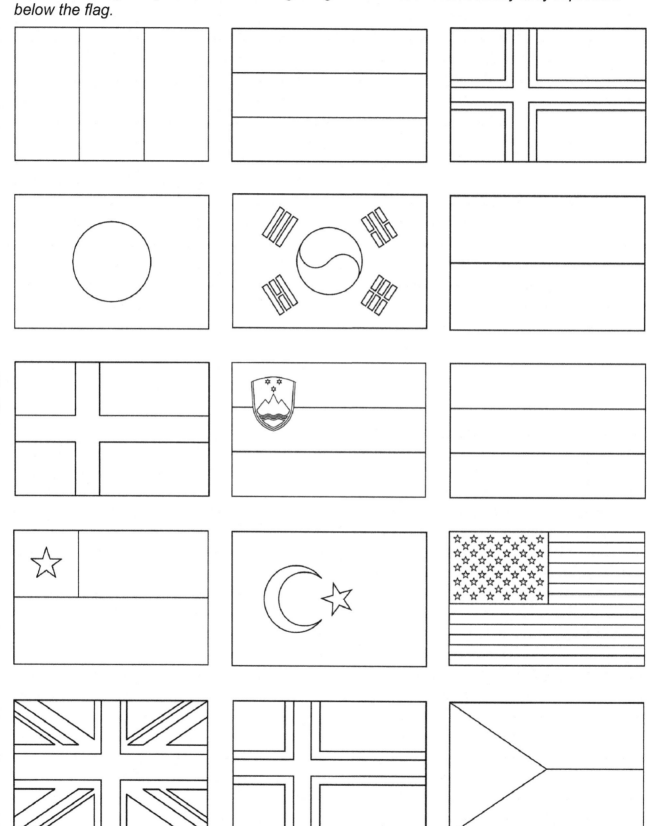

WORLD FLAGS

What other flags do you see during the games? Draw them here and write the name of the country below them.

UNIFORMS

Each country chooses a designer to create a uniform for their athletes to wear to the opening ceremony. They often choose uniforms that use their countries colors, and include images and themes that are important to their country. This may include symbols, special fabrics, or historical designs. It's fun to see what each athlete wears to best represent their country!

Which country had the best uniforms? _____

Which country's uniforms did you like the least? _____

What did your country's uniforms look like? _____

_____

_____

_____

DESIGN YOUR UNIFORM

Describe your Uniform. What materials did you use? What does the color and design mean? What special features did you include?

_____
_____
_____
_____
_____
_____
_____
_____

ALPINE SKIING

5 Men's Events (Downhill, Super-G, Giant Slalom, Slalom, Alpine Combined)
5 Women's Events (Downhill, Super-G, Giant Slalom, Slalom, Alpine Combined)
Alpine Team Event

Downhill skiing is the longest alpine skiing race in the games. The goal is to get down the mountain with the fastest time. Athletes are given one attempt to make it down the mountain, which is very steep and is covered in ice. The race includes turns, jumps and straightaways.

Skiers tend to use the "tuck" position in downhill events to allow them to pick up a lot of speed. Alpine skiers can go as fast as 90 - 140 kph as they move down the mountain!

THINGS TO KNOW

SLALOM
Slalom courses are short with sharp turns.

GATES
Slalom races include "gates" which are narrow sets of two poles that the skier goes through on their way down the mountain. The gates are moved to new locations for each "run" and practice runs are not allowed.

GIANT SLALOM
This race is similar to slalom except that the course is longer and the gates are farther apart to allow for faster speeds.

SUPERGIANT (SUPER-G)
This is an event that combines downhill and giant slalom events. The gates are placed farther apart, allowing skiers to go very quickly down the slope.

How fast is 90 Kilometers per Hour in Miles per Hour?

MY OBSERVATIONS

Watch at least one event for this sport. What is the most interesting thing you noticed about this sport? What do the competitors do? Who won the event(s) you watched? Share your observations. Do you enjoy watching it? Why or why not?

_____
_____
_____
_____
_____
_____
_____
_____
_____
_____
_____
_____
_____
_____
_____

AND THE MEDALISTS ARE...

EVENT: _____

GOLD: _____

SILVER: _____

BRONZE: _____

EVENT: _____

GOLD: _____

SILVER: _____

BRONZE: _____

FUN FACT

In 1998, skier Jean-Luc Cretier was the only competitor to safely ski past gate 8. All other skiers crashed at the gate, leaving him to take home the gold.

BIATHLON

5 Men's Events (Individual, Sprint, Pursuit, Mass Start, Relay)
5 Women's Events (Individual, Sprint, Pursuit, Mass Start, Relay)
1 Women's + Men's Mixed Relay

Biathlon combines cross-country skiing and shooting targets with rifles. This sport originated in Norway, where it was used as a training method for the military. During these events, the athletes strap their rifles on their backs, ski for the required distance, and then stop to shoot at the target. There are two different positions for athletes to shoot in. They can shoot while standing up on their skis, or while on their stomachs (prone).

Their scores are decided by how quickly they ski, and how accurately they shot the target. Each athlete must hit five targets, and they are penalized for each target they miss. If they get a penalty, they have to ski extra loops around the track.

THINGS TO KNOW

INDIVIDUAL- The athlete shoots four times, in the order of prone, standing, prone, standing, for a total of 20 targets.

SPRINT-The athlete shoots twice at each shooting line, once prone and once standing, for a total of 10 shots.

PURSUIT- The athlete who crosses the finish line first is the winner. There are four shooting bouts (two prone, two standing, in that order).

MASS START- All athletes start at the same time and the first across the finish line wins.

RELAY- For every round of five targets there are eight bullets available. If after eight bullets there are still misses, penalty loops must be taken.

If each missed target is a 150 meter penalty, how many meters will a relay team have to ski if they miss 4 targets?

MY OBSERVATIONS

Watch at least one event for this sport. What is the most interesting thing you noticed about this sport? What do the competitors do? Who won the event(s) you watched? Share your observations. Do you enjoy watching it? Why or why not?

_____
_____
_____
_____
_____
_____
_____
_____
_____
_____
_____
_____
_____
_____
_____

AND THE MEDALISTS ARE...

EVENT: _____
GOLD: _____
SILVER: _____
BRONZE: _____

EVENT: _____
GOLD: _____
SILVER: _____
BRONZE: _____

FUN FACT

This is the only sport in the Winter Games where an American athlete has never medaled. Maybe this year an American will win!

CROSS-COUNTRY SKIING

Cross-country is the oldest type of skiing. It originated in Norway, where people needed skis to hunt, trade, and collect firewood in the winter. Unlike other types of skiing, athletes don't need a special run or track to ski on. You can cross-country ski just about anywhere. As long as there is snow on the ground, you can cross-country ski!

Cross-country skiers race across a snow covered field to see who can do it with the shortest time. Many people think the field is flat, but it has equal uphill, level, and downhill segments. Cross-country skiing is one of the safest sports in the Winter Games, with less injuries than the other sports.

THINGS TO KNOW

SKATE SKIING- this is done on smooth, flat surfaces, and the skier moves a lot like an ice skater would across the snow, one foot at a time at an angle.

CLASSICAL SKIING- this is the most common way to cross-country ski and is used on prepared tracks with grooves or on rough terrain. One ski moves forward at a time in a striding or gliding motion.

If a skier travels 40 mph on the downhills, and 20 mph on the flat surfaces, how quickly would they finish an 80 mile race that is half flat and half downhill?

MY OBSERVATIONS

Watch at least one event for this sport. What is the most interesting thing you noticed about this sport? What do the competitors do? Who won the event(s) you watched? Share your observations. Do you enjoy watching it? Why or why not?

_____
_____
_____
_____
_____
_____
_____
_____
_____
_____
_____
_____
_____
_____
_____
_____
_____
_____

AND THE MEDALISTS ARE...

EVENT: _____
GOLD: _____
SILVER: _____
BRONZE: _____

EVENT _____
GOLD: _____
SILVER: _____
BRONZE: _____

FUN FACT

In 2014, Sadie and Erik Bjornsen both qualified for the American team. They are a brother/sister duo from Alaska. Sadie is competing again this year!

FREESTYLE SKIING

5 Men's Events (Aerials, Moguls, Ski Cross, Ski Halfpipe, Ski Slopestyle)
5 Women's Events (Aerials, Moguls, Ski Cross, Ski Halfpipe, Ski Slopestyle)

Freestyle Skiing is one of the newest sports in the Winter Games, but people have been flipping and spinning on their skis since the 1920s. Some people say the freestyle events are like watching a "circus on the snow" because the skiers do things like back-flips, twists, spins and other tricks through the air as they ski down the mountain.

Freestyle skis tend to be much shorter than skis used in other sports, which allows the athlete more freedom of movement as they perform their tricks. This event is not for the faint of heart, slopes are very steep, and there are jumps and bumps intended to help the athlete launch themselves very high in the air.

THINGS TO KNOW

MOGULS: a downhill race with artificially created "bumps" in the snow to jump/turn on.

AERIALS: the skier will go ski off jumps in order to do flips and twists in the air.

SKI CROSS: Four athletes race on the course at the same time and do jumps and other tricks as they meet different obstacles on their path.

SKI HALFPIPE: the athlete does jumps and turns on a halfpipe slope.

SKI SLOPESTYLE: the skier can choose their obstacles to create a run with many jumps and interesting obstacles. They are rated on difficultly, skill, and the height they get on their jumps.

Moguls skis are 180 cm long and aerial skis are 160 cm long. What percentage shorter are aerial skis than mogul skis?

MY OBSERVATIONS

Watch at least one event for this sport. What is the most interesting thing you noticed about this sport? What do the competitors do? Who won the event(s) you watched? Share your observations. Do you enjoy watching it? Why or why not?

_____

_____

_____

_____

_____

_____

_____

_____

_____

_____

_____

_____

_____

_____

_____

_____

AND THE MEDALISTS ARE...

EVENT: _____

GOLD: _____

SILVER: _____

BRONZE: _____

EVENT: _____

GOLD: _____

SILVER: _____

BRONZE: _____

FUN FACT

Freestyle Skiing is also called "hot dog skiing" because the skiers who first competed were known as "hot dogs" on the slopes.

NORDIC COMBINED

Individual Gundersen Normal Hill
Individual Gundersen Large Hill
Team Gundersen Large Hill

This sport combines cross-country skiing and ski jumping. The Nordic Combined started at a ski festival in 1982 in Sweden. It became very popular, and in the 1920s, King Olav V of Norway even competed. It has been a part of the Winter Games from the very first games.

This is one of the hardest ski disciplines, because not only do athletes need to have the strength and stamina to cross country ski, they have to have to be brave enough and talented enough to do the ski jump.

Only men compete in this sport at the Winter Games, however, in 2017 the United States held the first Women's Nordic Combined National Championships. The games evolve over time, and many female athletes are hoping to see women compete in this sport in future games.

THINGS TO KNOW

INRUN- The portion of the jump during which the athlete travels down the ramp.

TAKEOFF- At the end of the inrun, the moment where the jumper takes flight.

K POINT- The distance from the takeoff that is equivalent to the height of the hill. For the large hill in PyeongChang, the K Point is 125 meters from the takeoff; for the normal hill, it is 95 meters. The K Point determines the amount of distance points awarded to a jump.

OUTRUN- The flat area at the bottom of the hill where skiers decelerate and stop.

If a skier in Pyeongchang competes in the Large Hill and lands some 95 meters in the outrun area, what is the total distance traveled from takeoff to initial landing?

MY OBSERVATIONS

Watch at least one event for this sport. What is the most interesting thing you noticed about this sport? What do the competitors do? Who won the event(s) you watched? Share your observations. Do you enjoy watching it? Why or why not?

_____
_____
_____
_____
_____
_____
_____
_____
_____
_____
_____
_____
_____
_____
_____
_____

AND THE MEDALISTS ARE...

EVENT: _____

GOLD: _____

SILVER: _____

BRONZE: _____

EVENT: _____

GOLD: _____

SILVER: _____

BRONZE: _____

FUN FACT

"Ski" is a Nordic word which comes from the Old Norse word "skid" which means a split length of wood.

SKI JUMPING

3 Men's Events (Normal Hill Individual, Large Hill Individual, Men's Team)
1 Women's Event (Normal Hill Individual)

Ski Jumping is a sport where the skier glides down a steep ramp to jump as far and as high as they can and still land gracefully. Skiers race down the hill at 90 km/h and then launch into the air.

There are five judges watching each event to determine the athletes score. They give (and take away) points for the posture of the athlete as they fly through the air, and their posture and gracefulness when they land in the landing section. These scores are added to the score they receive from their distance. The highest and lowest scores are thrown out, and then they average the middle three scores to get the final results.

THINGS TO KNOW

KONGSBERGER TECHNIQUE- the original jumping style. Athletes jumped with the upper body bent at the hips, leaning forward, with arms extended at the front (Superman style) with the skis parallel to each other.

V-POSITION- The modern position of the skis most jumpers use.. The skis are touching or nearly touching at the back, and are spread apart at the front to form a "V." The athlete holds his hands behind him, close to his body.

TELEMARK POSITION- Landing with one ski in front of the other while leaning forward.

If a jumper receives these scores for style in his or her jump, what will their total style score be?

17 18.5 17.5 19 and 20

MY OBSERVATIONS

Watch at least one event for this sport. What is the most interesting thing you noticed about this sport? What do the competitors do? Who won the event(s) you watched? Share your observations. Do you enjoy watching it? Why or why not?

_____
_____
_____
_____
_____
_____
_____
_____
_____
_____
_____
_____
_____
_____
_____
_____
_____

AND THE MEDALISTS ARE...

EVENT: _____
GOLD: _____
SILVER: _____
BRONZE: _____

EVENT _____
GOLD: _____
SILVER: _____
BRONZE: _____

FUN FACT

Ski Jumping is the most popular sport in the Winter Games . . . why do you think that is? Is it your favorite sport?

SNOWBOARD

5 Men's Events (Parallel Giant Slalom, Halfpipe, Snowboard Cross, Slopestyle, Big Air)
5 Women's Events (Parallel Giant Slalom, Halfpipe, Snowboard Cross, Slopestyle, Big Air)

Snowboarding combines parts of skiing, surfing and skateboarding. It's a relatively new sport in the games, making its first appearance in 1998. Snowboarding started in the 1960s in the United States, but not everyone was excited about it. Many skiers were upset that snowboarders were invading "their" mountains, but overtime, they grew to accept the sport.

There are two types of snowboarding in the 2018 Winter Games, alpine snowboarding (on groomed slopes) and freestyle snowboarding. The only Alpine event for snowboard is the Parallel Giant Slalom, where two snowboarders go down the slope at the same time, navigating through gates, in a race to see who can get the bottom first.

THINGS TO KNOW

AIR- A rider gets "air" when the snowboarder launches above the lip of the halfpipe.

GRAB- The way an athlete grabs and holds their snowboard with their hand(s) during a trick. This shows control and adds to a rider's personal style. There are many different types of grabs.

JIB- A surface other than snow, such as a rail or box.

STANCE- The position of the rider's feet on the snowboard. All riders are considered either regular-footed (left foot forward) or goofy-footed (right foot forward).

If the first Winter Games which allowed snowboarding was 1998, how many Winter Games has there been since then?

MY OBSERVATIONS

Watch at least one event for this sport. What is the most interesting thing you noticed about this sport? What do the competitors do? Who won the event(s) you watched? Share your observations. Do you enjoy watching it? Why or why not?

_____

_____

_____

_____

_____

_____

_____

_____

_____

_____

_____

_____

_____

_____

_____

AND THE MEDALISTS ARE...

EVENT: _____

GOLD: _____

SILVER: _____

BRONZE: _____

EVENT: _____

GOLD: _____

SILVER: _____

BRONZE: _____

FUN FACT

The halfpipe used in the Winter Games has walls that are 22 feet tall on the sides!

SPEED SKATING

7 Men's Events (500m, 1,000m, 1,500m, 5,000m, 10,000m, Mass Start, Team Pursuit)
7 Women's Events (500m, 1,000m, 1,500m, 3,000m, 5,000m, Mass Start, Team Pursuit)
There are also 8 Short Track Speed Skating Events for Men and Women

Speed skating originated in the Netherlands, when people would skate along the canals between villages in the 13th century. Speed Skating was one of the events in the first Winter Games in 1924. Women were not allowed to compete in the speed skating events until 1960.

The speed skating track is 400m long, and every skater is required to stay in their own lane. Because the inner track is shorter than the outer track, skaters are supposed to change lanes at a specific spot in the circle to make sure they all skate the same distance.

Short track races are done "pack style" where skaters are not required to stay in their own lane. The track is much shorter than the standard speed skating track and the first person across the finish line wins.

THINGS TO KNOW

BACKSTRETCH- The straight section of the track where the skaters change lanes to ensure all skaters travel the same distance.

BLOCKS- Barriers placed on the track to show where the boundaries are. The athletes must skate outside the blocks at all times.

CORNERING TECHNIQUE- One arm is swung diagonally to help the skater balance, while the other arm is swung to obtain speed, or held behind the back to conserve energy.

The coastline of the Netherlands is 451 kilometers. How long would it take a speed skater going 60 k/h to travel the coast?

MY OBSERVATIONS

Watch at least one event for this sport. What is the most interesting thing you noticed about this sport? What do the competitors do? Who won the event(s) you watched? Share your observations. Do you enjoy watching it? Why or why not?

_____

_____

_____

_____

_____

_____

_____

_____

_____

_____

_____

_____

_____

_____

_____

_____

_____

AND THE MEDALISTS ARE...

EVENT: _____

GOLD: _____

SILVER: _____

BRONZE: _____

EVENT: _____

GOLD: _____

SILVER: _____

BRONZE: _____

FUN FACT

The first Winter Games champion was American Charles Jewtraw who won the gold in the 500 meter speed skating event.

FIGURE SKATING

5 Events:
Men Single Skating, Womens Single Skating,
Pair Skating, Ice Dance, Team Event

Figure skating is a very popular sport in the Winter Games. Athletes wear elaborate costumes, and skate on ice to music. The skaters dance on the ice, do jumps and spins, and are judged on the accuracy of their moves as well as how difficult the moves they attempt are.

In the Pairs events, the men throw the women so they can jump in the air, lift the woman over their head while skating, do "death spirals" (where the woman is spin around parallel to the ice), and spin together.

In the Ice Dance events, the man and woman must stay together while doing complicated dance steps. They cannot be apart from each other for more than 5 seconds at a time.

THINGS TO KNOW

AXEL - a jump from the forward outside edge of one skate to the backward outside edge of the other skate, with one and a half turns in the air.

LUTZ - a jump from the backward outside edge of one skate to the backward outside edge of the other skate, with one or more full turns in the air.

TOE LOOP - a jump, started with the help of the supporting foot, in which the skater makes a full turn in the air, taking off from and landing on the outside edge of the same foot.

If a skater does 8 rotations in a death spiral, how many total degrees did they spin?

MY OBSERVATIONS

Watch at least one event for this sport. What is the most interesting thing you noticed about this sport? What do the competitors do? Who won the event(s) you watched? Share your observations. Do you enjoy watching it? Why or why not?

_____
_____
_____
_____
_____
_____
_____
_____
_____
_____
_____
_____
_____
_____
_____
_____

AND THE MEDALISTS ARE...

EVENT: _____

GOLD: _____

SILVER: _____

BRONZE: _____

EVENT: _____

GOLD: _____

SILVER: _____

BRONZE: _____

FUN FACT

In 1998, 15 year old Tara Lipinski became the youngest woman ever to win an gold figure skating medal.

ICE HOCKEY

Men's and Women's Tournaments

Ice Hockey is a favorite for many people in the Winter Games, maybe because it's fun to watch such a large team win games! In the tournaments, a game will be played between two teams, with the winners moving on to the next round, until there is only one winner left.

Games last three twenty minute periods, with short breaks between them. The goal is to get the puck into the opponents net. The game is played on an ice rink, with the players in skates. They wear padding to protect their bodies from the rough sport, which includes "checking" (bumping into each other) as they fight for the puck and try to get goals.

WORDS TO KNOW

GOAL- When the puck is inside the goal net.

SAVE- any shot on goal which is stopped by the goalie.

POWER PLAY- When one team has the advantage by having more skaters on the ice because their opponent has a penalty for breaking the rules.

ICING- Icing is called when teams shoot the puck from anywhere behind the red line at center ice and it travels, untouched by any player, across the opposite end goal line, also known as the icing line.

HAT TRICK- when a player scores three or more goals in a game.

If each team has 22 players, and 12 countries participate in the Men's and Women's tournament, how many total hockey players are there?

MY OBSERVATIONS

Watch at least one event for this sport. What is the most interesting thing you noticed about this sport? What do the competitors do? Who won the event(s) you watched? Share your observations. Do you enjoy watching it? Why or why not?

_____
_____
_____
_____
_____
_____
_____
_____
_____
_____
_____
_____
_____
_____
_____
_____

AND THE MEDALISTS ARE...

EVENT: _____

GOLD: _____

SILVER: _____

BRONZE: _____

EVENT: _____

GOLD: _____

SILVER: _____

BRONZE: _____

FUN FACT

In 1980, the U.S. Men's Ice Hockey team defeated the Soviet Team despite going into the game as underdogs. The win was called a "Miracle on Ice."

CURLING

Curling is a team sport that is played on a rectangular ice rink. There are five players on each team, four who are on the ice, and one who is an alternate (and can step into play if one of the other players can't play).

Curling games are very long. They include ten ends, and last almost three hours. The two teams take turns to throw eight stones each (each player will throw two stones). Stones are thrown one at a time and the players will brush the ice with the broom to help the stone move where they want it to go. After they have thrown all sixteen stones, the "end" is complete.

Curling is also called "The Roaring Game" because the granite stones, which weigh 44 pounds each, make a loud roaring sound as they move across the bumpy ice.

THINGS TO KNOW

BROOM- There are two types of brooms used for curling, "push brooms" and long bristled brooms.

ICE- The ice has rough water droplets on it and is called "pebbled ice", this surface helps the stone's grip and leads to more consistent curling.

RINK- The rink is 42.07m long and 4.28m wide with a target (also called a house) at either end.

STONE- a curling rock is made of rare, dense polished granite that comes from Scotland.

What are the dimensions of a curling rink in feet?

MY OBSERVATIONS

Watch at least one event for this sport. What is the most interesting thing you noticed about this sport? What do the competitors do? Who won the event(s) you watched? Share your observations. Do you enjoy watching it? Why or why not?

_____
_____
_____
_____
_____
_____
_____
_____
_____
_____
_____
_____
_____
_____
_____
_____

AND THE MEDALISTS ARE...

EVENT: _____
GOLD: _____
SILVER: _____
BRONZE: _____

EVENT: _____
GOLD: _____
SILVER: _____
BRONZE: _____

FUN FACT

The oldest person to ever win an curling medal is British Curler Robin Walsh, who was 54.

BOB SLED

2-man, 4-man and Women's Events

The first bobsled was made by tying two skeleton sleds together and adding a steering rope. Over time, sides were added to the sled to protect the passengers from the cold, wet snow and to make them more safe.

A Bobsled race starts with a push start at the top of the track. During the bobsled race, the pilot uses a rope inside the sled to control how it goes around the turns. A sledder called the brakeman pulls the brake to stop the sled after it has passed the finish line. During the four-man race, there are two extra teammates who help with the push start to make the sled go faster.

The pressure bobsledders feel while going around the curves on the track is nearly four times the force of gravity, and the bobsleigh reaches an average maximum speed of 135Km an hour. Bobsled teams have to carefully maneuver around turns without slowing down, because the race is often decided by less than a second.

THINGS TO KNOW

WEIGHT LIMITS- In the 1950s, many Bob Sled teams were "heavy weights" because heavy sleds went down the track much faster than light sleds. Today, there are strict weight limits for the sleds and the riders.

LABYRINTH A combination of three or four small curves with little or no straightaway between them.

What is the difference in time between the fastest Bob Sled race you watched, and the slowest?

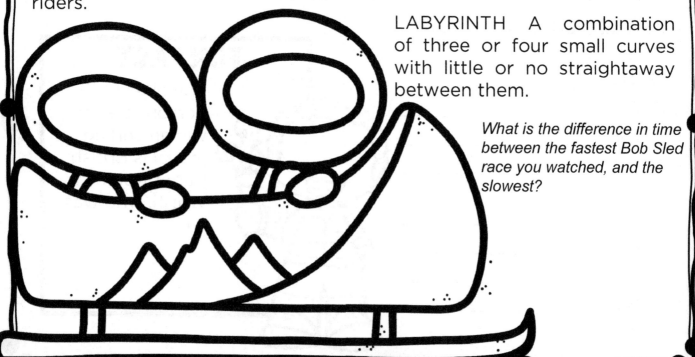

MY OBSERVATIONS

Watch at least one event for this sport. What is the most interesting thing you noticed about this sport? What do the competitors do? Who won the event(s) you watched? Share your observations. Do you enjoy watching it? Why or why not?

_____
_____
_____
_____
_____
_____
_____
_____
_____
_____
_____
_____
_____
_____
_____
_____

AND THE MEDALISTS ARE...

EVENT: _____
GOLD: _____
SILVER: _____
BRONZE: _____

EVENT: _____
GOLD: _____
SILVER: _____
BRONZE: _____

FUN FACT

The movie "Cool Runnings" is inspired by the true story of the 1988 Jamaican Bobsled Team. Much of the story is fiction, the real time was made up of Army soldiers.

LUGE

Men's Singles
Women's Singles
Doubles & Team Relay

The luge is a small sled - the athlete lays down on their back and goes down the track feet first. The luge races are done on the same track as the bobsled and include many curves.

Luge racers slide down the track at 140 kilometers per hour and their sleds do not have breaks. Luge drivers steer by using subtle body movements, leaning to change their course.

Their sleds do not include any protective sides, which makes this a very dangerous sport. Because they travel so quickly, races are timed to one thousandth of a second. Races are often very close. This competition can be done with one or two athletes. If two sledders are riding, the larger athlete lays down on top of the smaller athlete.

WORDS TO KNOW

BOOTIE- The name for a luge racing shoe

LINE- The fastest route down the track.

POD- The seat for the athlete.

If a Luge sledder can travel 140 kilometers per hour, and the Hallasan mountain in South Korea is 1,950 meters tall, how long would it take to sled down it, if the sledder had a straight path?

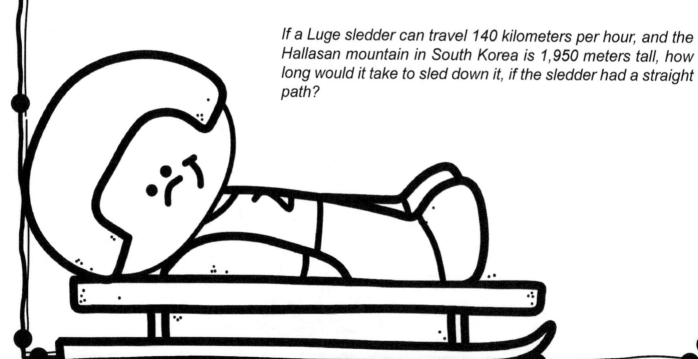

MY OBSERVATIONS

Watch at least one event for this sport. What is the most interesting thing you noticed about this sport? What do the competitors do? Who won the event(s) you watched? Share your observations. Do you enjoy watching it? Why or why not?

_____

_____

_____

_____

_____

_____

_____

_____

_____

_____

_____

_____

_____

_____

AND THE MEDALISTS ARE...

EVENT: _____

GOLD: _____

SILVER: _____

BRONZE: _____

EVENT: _____

GOLD: _____

SILVER: _____

BRONZE: _____

FUN FACT

The women's luge track is shorter and has fewer curves than the men's track. Women can compete in the doubles contest, but it's rare that they do.

SKELETON
Men's and Women's Events

The skeleton is a type of toboggan that was used by Native Americans to transport goods for trade in the winter. It became a part of the Winter Games at the second games in 1928. It hasn't always been a part of the games though - many found it to be too dangerous, and it didn't become a standard part of the games until 2002.

In this event, sledders travel on their stomachs, head-first, down the track. The pressure felt by the athlete when turning the curve is almost four times the force of gravity. They travel almost 120 kilometers per hour, and have very little protection other than their helmet if something goes wrong.

This is a very dangerous sport, but it's very fun to watch!

THINGS TO KNOW

GROOVE- Skeleton athletes steer by moving their bodies slightly while sliding down the track. Before they jump on their sled, it is in grooves at the top of the track to help it stay stable.

HEAT- A single run down the track during a race. All races will do four heats.

SLIDER- Another name for a skeleton athlete.

TOBOGGAN- The sled used in skeleton.

LINE- The fastest route down the track. A high line takes the sled close to the top lip of a turn, while a low line takes the sled closer to the bottom of a turn.

If there are 36 skeleton heats spaced evenly over 9 hours of competition in a single day, how many heats are run per hour?

MY OBSERVATIONS

Watch at least one event for this sport. What is the most interesting thing you noticed about this sport? What do the competitors do? Who won the event(s) you watched? Share your observations. Do you enjoy watching it? Why or why not?

_____
_____
_____
_____
_____
_____
_____
_____
_____
_____
_____
_____
_____
_____
_____
_____
_____
_____

AND THE MEDALISTS ARE...

EVENT: _____
GOLD: _____
SILVER: _____
BRONZE: _____

EVENT: _____
GOLD: _____
SILVER: _____
BRONZE: _____

FUN FACT

One of the coolest things to look for during the Skeleton competition is the different designs of the riders helmets. Each one is unique!

CROSSWORD

ACROSS

4) The skier will go ski off jumps to perform flips and twists in the air.
5) A jump, started with the help of the supporting foot, in which the skater makes a full turn in the air, taking off from and landing on the outside edge of the same foot.
7) A downhill race with artificially created "bumps" in the snow to jump/turn on.
12) The sport that combines cross-country skiing with rifle shooting.
13) The way an athlete grabs and holds their snowboard with their hand(s) during a trick.
14) The sled used in skeleton.
15) Done on smooth, flat surfaces. The skier moves a lot like an ice skater would across the snow, one foot at a time at an angle.
16) When a hockey player scores three or more goals in a game.
17) Narrow sets of two poles that the skier goes through on their way down the mountain.

DOWN

1) Another name for a curling rock.
2) Short ski courses with sharp turns.
3) The name for a luge racing shoe.
6) When one hockey team has the advantage by having more skaters on the ice because their opponent has a penalty for breaking the rules.
8) A combination of three or four small curves on a bobsled track with little or no straightaway between them.
9) The modern position of the skis most jumpers use.
10) The distance from the takeoff that is equivalent to the height of the hill.
11) A surface other than snow, such as a rail or box.
12) The straight section of the track in which the speed skaters change lanes to ensure all skaters travel the same distance.
18) A jump from the forward outside edge of one skate to the backward outside edge of the other skate, with one and a half turns in the air.

MEDALS

In 2018, 102 total medals will be awarded in the 15 different sports. Did you know that the fourth place winner earns an diploma? Gold, Silver and Bronze medal winners bring home their medal and a diploma.

Use the PyeongChang official medal page to find the answers to these questions

What inspired the design of this year's medals?

_____

What does the texture represent?

_____

How much does the gold medal weigh?

_____

What kind of fabric are the medals hung on?

_____

_____

What does the back of the medals say?

_____

_____

What do you think of this year's design? What would you have done differently?

_____

_____

_____

_____

_____

_____

What does the 2018 Winter Gold Medal look like? Color it here.

MEDAL GRAPHING

Use the following pages to create a bar graph of the medals awarded. Use three different colors to graph gold, silver and bronze medals. When you are finished graphing, return to this page to answer these questions.

1. Which country received the most overall medals?

_____

2. Which country received the most gold medals?

_____

3. Which country received the most silver medals?

_____

4. Which country received the most bronze medals?

_____

5. What percentage of the overall gold medals awarded went to the country who won the most medals?

_____

6. What percentage of the overall gold medals did your country take home?

_____

Look at medal standings for each sport on the Internet to answer these questions:

7. How many medals total were given out in your favorite sport?

_____

8. How many athletes competed in your favorite sport?

_____

9. What is the ratio of medals to competitors in your favorite sport? How would you write that ratio as a percentage?

_____

TITLE: _____

NUMBER OF MEDALS

COUNTRY

TITLE: _____

NUMBER OF MEDALS

COUNTRY

THE CLOSING CEREMONY

The closing ceremony brings people from all over the world together. You'll see cultural performances, the parade of athletes, and watch the victory ceremony. They also extinguish the torch flame at this ceremony.

Share your favorite part of the closing ceremony:

_____
_____
_____
_____
_____
_____
_____
_____
_____

REFLECTIONS

What was your favorite moment of the 2018 Winter Games? Describe it so you'll remember it!

_____

_____

_____

_____

_____

_____

_____

_____

_____

_____

_____

_____

If you were to compete in the Winter Games, which event would you want to enter and why? What would you need to do to prepare to compete?

_____

_____

_____

_____

_____

_____

_____

_____

_____

_____

_____

_____

EXTRA CRAFTS & ACTIVITIES

1. Host your own children's Winter Games!

   Plan events for your siblings, classmates or friends to participate in. Some ideas include: sled races, relay races, jumping contests, three-legged team races (anything you can dream up!)

   Create medals to hand out to winners, and choose someone to judge the contests.

   Include an Opening Ceremony (you could have a talent show as a part of the cultural performances and sing your national anthem) and a Closing Ceremony to present the medals.

2. Enjoy dinner around the world.

   Do some research to see what dishes are popular in the countries who won gold medals. Celebrate their win by cooking those dishes. You can decorate the dining table by coloring flags from the winning country.

3. Create your own special "uniform" to watch the Winter Games in.

   Grab a white T-shirt and fabric markers and create a special design to represent your country.

4. Design your own medals out of modeling clay.

   Use polymer clay (available at craft stores) to create medals you can bake and keep! Make sure to create a hole in your medal with a straw before baking so you can string it on a ribbon to wear.

5. Write a research report.

   Research the country who won the most medals in your favorite sport. Include information on the geography, culture, language, history, landmarks and common foods. If you like, you can create a travel brochure for the country to encourage people to visit it.

6. Have a Toga Party!

Watch the Winter Games in white togas made of sheets as a way to honor the Greeks.

7. Create Olive Branch Wreaths to wear

Remove the center from a paper plate, and decorate it with construction paper leaves.

8. Make a flag banner.

How many different flags did you see during the opening ceremony? Color flags on pieces of paper, and hang them as a banner around your home.

8. Create the Winter Games rings out of Legos.

Can you build the Winter Games rings out of Lego bricks? Give it a try! You can also craft them out of paper towel tubes, donuts (add colored frosting) or paper! Research what the different colored rings mean and write a paragraph about them.

10. Learn about the physics of the Winter Games

With your parents help, look up the physics of the winter sports on YouTube.

11. Create an Ice Luge/Bob Sled race track

Use Hot Wheels tracks, plastic, or some other smooth material to create a track, and then race ice cubes down it. Run experiments to see what travels faster - heavier/larger ice cubes, or smaller ones? Test different types of "sleds" down your track, and different track angles/layouts as well.

**What other crafts & activities can you come up with?
Use your imagination!**

ANSWER KEY

THE FIRST ATHLETES

Fill in the blanks using these words: wreaths, male, youth, woman, chariot, olive, Rome, Kroton, rumored, victory

During the ancient games, athletes had to be three things. They had to be **male**, from Greece, and born free. After Greece was conquered by **Rome**, Romans were able to join in the games as well. Winners were given **wreaths** made of olive branches to wear.

ASTYLOS OF KROTON- Astylos was a runner who won six victory **olive** wreaths in three different Olympiads. After his first Olympiad, he competed for Syracuse instead of Kroton, so the people of **Kroton** destroyed his statue.

MILON OF KROTON- Milon was a wrestling champion and one of the most famous ancient Olympians. He won first as a **youth**, and then went on to compete five more time as an adult.

KYNISKA OF SPARTA- Kyniska was the first **woman** to be listed as an victor. She did not compete, but she owned the horse who won the **chariot** race, and the owner, not the rider, was listed as the victor.

LEONIDAS OF RHODES- Leonidas is a famous runner. He ran in three different events in four different Olympiads, winning a total of 12 **victory** wreaths.

MELANKOMAS OF KARIA- Melankomas was a boxer, who was said to win his matches without ever being hit, or hitting anyone else. It is **rumored** that he won a match by holding his arms out for two days without lowering them.

WORD SEARCH

Find these words:

RUNNING
WRESTLING
BOXING
PANKRATION
CHARIOT
PENTATHLON
JAVELIN
DISCUS
GYMNASIUM
PALAESTRA
OLYMPIAD
OLYMPIA

OLYMPICS
ZEUS
HERCULES
KRONOS
ASTYLOS
OLIVE
MILON
KYNISKA
LEONIDAS
MELANKOMAS
GREECE
HERO

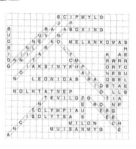

FUN WITH GREEK ROOTS

Read the root word and its meaning. Then, come up with a word you know that includes the root word. Highlight the root. Use a dictionary or the internet for help if needed.

ROOT	MEANING	WORDS I KNOW
anthropo	man; human; humanity	anthropology
auto	self	automobile
bio	life	biology
chron	time	chronological
dys	bad; hard; unlucky	dysfunctional
gram	thing written	grammar
hydr	water	dehydrated
hypo	below; beneath	astronomy
logy	study of	meteorology
meter/metr	measure	microscopic
micro	small	monotheistic
mono	one	metamorphosis
morph	form, shape	philanthropy
phil	love	arachnophobia
phobia	fear	photography
photo/phos	light	thermal
therm	heat	

TORCH WORD PROBLEMS

1. The flame traveled a total of 2,018 Kilometers. How far is that same distance in miles?

2018 km = 1253.93 Miles.

2. 7,500 different torch bearers carried the flame. If each torch bearer carried the flame the same amount of distance, how far would each torch bearer need to carry the flame?

2018/7500=.269 km OR 1253.93/7500=.167 Miles.

3. There are 75,000,000 people living in Korea. The torch stopped in 45 Korean cities. If an equal number of Korean residents traveled to see the torch at each stop it made (one view per resident), how many people would be watching the torch pass through Incheon on its first stop?

75000000/45=1,666,666.67 people per stop

4. The torch relay this year took a total of 109 days! A Luge can reach the speed of 140 MPH. If the torch was carried by Luge instead of by foot, how long would it take to travel the 2,018 Kilometers?

First convert 2018 km to miles then use R*T=D to solve.
1253.93/140=8.95 Days.

Go for the Gold!

Helpful Hint!
1 mile =
1.6 Kilometers

THE OFFICIAL TORCH OF 2018

A new torch is designed for each new Games. This year, the torch has new features designed to help it stay lit while it travels through the extreme weather in South Korea.

Visit the Official 2018 Torch Website to help you answer these questions.

1. What does the pentagon shape represent?
Pentagon shapes at the top and bottom parts symbolize the five continents of the world.

2. What special features does the torch include to help it stay lit?
The torch has a combustion compartment with four separate walls to protect from the wind, an umbrella-like cover, and a design to allow air circulation.

3. How much wind can the torch withstand?
Max. wind speed
35m/s

4. How big is the torch? What does its size represent?
The torch is 700 mm tall to represent the host city being 700 meters above sea level.

5. What do the stars on the torch represent?
Peace and harmony.

ABOUT SOUTH KOREA

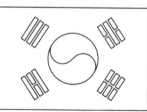

Use an atlas or look on the Internet to help you find the following answers:

Official Name: **Republic of Korea**

Type of Government: **Republic**

Capital: **Seoul**

Population: **49,039,986**

Language: **Korean**

Religion: **Confucianism**

Currency: **Won**

Tallest Mountain: **Hallasan**

Important Rivers: **Han, Kum, Naktong**

Largest City: **Seoul**

How large is South Korea? **38,691 mi² (about 1/3 the size of California)**

THE KOREAN WAR

Fill in the blanks using these words: million, wildlife, tensions, population, North, countries, safe, communist, isolated, war, border.

The official name of South Korea is "The Republic of Korea" (ROK). South Korea does not acknowledge that <u>North</u> Korea is a separate country, despite the <u>tensions</u> between the two nations.

In 1950, <u>communist</u> forces from North Korea invaded the South, which started the Korean War. Between 1950-1953, more than two and a half <u>million</u> people died. The war never officially ended. Instead, a "demilitarized zone" (DMZ) was set up between the <u>countries</u> and to this day, soldiers from each country stand at that line, prepared for another <u>war</u>.

The DMZ has become something like a <u>wildlife</u> preserve, and has been untouched for more than 60 years. Most of the country has buildings because of the large <u>population</u> and small size, so this preserved wilderness is important to many people. When the war ends, many people hope to make the DMZ a permanent "peace park."

North Korea is completely <u>isolated</u> from South Korea, and some Korean families have been unable to see or speak to each other for years because no one is allowed to cross the <u>border</u> between North and South Korea.

Despite this, South Korea is a very <u>safe</u> country and many South Koreans don't worry about the war on a daily basis.

GREETINGS AROUND THE WORLD

How to say "Hello" in 20 languages.

Which country would you use these words in?

BONJOUR - French <u>France, Belgium, Switzerland</u>

HOLA - Spanish <u>Spain, many central and south American countries</u>

GUTEN TAG - German <u>Germany, Austria and Switzerland</u>

CIAO - Italian <u>Italy</u>

OLA - Portuguese <u>Portugal and Brazil</u>

NAMASTE - Hindi <u>Northern India and Nepal</u>

SALAAM - Persian (Farsi) <u>Iran, Afghanistan, Tajikistan</u>

ZDRAS-TVUY-TE - Russian <u>Russia, Kazakhstan</u>

KONNICHIWA - Japanese <u>Japan</u>

AHN-YOUNG-HA-SE-YO - Korean <u>North and South Korea</u>

MERHABA - Turkish <u>Turkey and Cyprus</u>

SAIN BAINUU- Mongolian <u>Mongolia</u>

SALEMETSIZ BE? - Kazakh <u>Kazakhstan</u>

SZIA - Hungarian <u>Hungary</u>

MARHABA - Arabic <u>North Africa and the Middle East</u>

SALAMA ALEIKUM - Hausa <u>Niger and Northern Nigeria</u>

JAMBO - Swahili <u>Tanzania, Uganda and Kenya</u>

NI HAU - Mandarin <u>China</u>

NAY HOH - Cantonese (Yue) <u>Southern China</u>

HALO - Bahase Indonesia <u>Indonesia</u>

CROSSWORD

MEDALS

In 2018, 102 total medals will be awarded in 15 different disciplines. Did you know that the fourth place winner earns an diploma? Gold, Silver and Bronze medal winners bring home their medal and a diploma.

Use the PyeongChang official medal page to find the answers to these questions

What inspired the design of this years medals?
The texture of tree trunks

What does the texture represent?
diagonal lines reflect both the history of the games and the determination of the participants

How much does the gold medal weigh?
586 grams

What kind of fabric are the medals hung on?
Traditional South Korean fabric embroidered with Hangeul patterns

What does the 2018 Winter Gold Medal look like? Color it here.

What does the back of the medals say?
The sport, event and the PyeongChang 2018 emblem

What do you think of this year's design? What would you have done differently?

_____

_____

_____

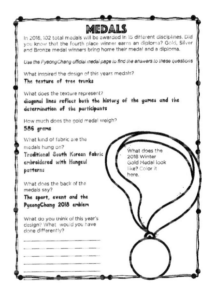

Sport Word Problem Answers:

Cross Country: 3 Hours
Biathlon: 600 meters
Alpine Skiing: 55.92 mph
Freestyle Skiing: 11.11% smaller
Nordic Combined: 220 meters
Ski Jumping: 18.33
Snowboarding: 5
Speed Skating: 7.52 hours
Figure Skating: 2880 degrees
Hockey: 528 players
Curling: 138.03 ft by 14.04 ft.
Luge: .014 hours
Bob Sled: Answers will vary.
Skeleton: 4

CPSIA information can be obtained
at www.ICGtesting.com
Printed in the USA
BVOW07s2000070218

507552BV00009B/241/P

9 781983 692079